HIT THE GROUND KNEELING

SEEING LEADERSHIP DIFFERENTLY

HIT THE GROUND KNEELING

SEEING LEADERSHIP DIFFERENTLY

STEPHEN COTTRELL

CHURCH HOUSE
PUBLISHING

Church House Publishing
Church House
Great Smith Street
London SW1P 3AZ

Tel: 020 7898 1451
Fax: 020 7898 1449

ISBN 978 0 7151 4162 5

Published 2008 by Church House Publishing

The opinions expressed in this book are those of the author and do not necessarily reflect the official policy of the General Synod or The Archbishops' Council of the Church of England.

The Scripture quotations contained herein are from The New Revised Standard Version of the Bible, Anglicized Edition, copyright © 1989, 1995 by the Division of Christian Education of the National Council of the Churches of Christ in the United States of America, and are used by permission. All rights reserved.

Printed in England by Cromwell Press Ltd, Trowbridge, Wiltshire

Desire without knowledge is not good, and one who moves too hurriedly misses the way.

Proverbs 19.2

Blessed are you if you reflect before you act and laugh before you reflect; you will avoid doing many stupid things.

Bernardo Olivera OCSO

The parable of the trees

The trees once went out
   to anoint a king over themselves.
So they said to the olive tree,
   'Reign over us.'
The olive tree answered them,
   'Shall I stop producing my rich oil
   by which gods and mortals are honoured,
   and go to sway over the trees?'
Then the trees said to the fig tree,
   'You come and reign over us.'
But the fig tree answered them,
   'Shall I stop producing my sweetness
   and my delicious fruit,
   and go to sway over the trees?'
Then the trees said to the vine,
   'You come and reign over us.'
But the vine said to them,
   'Shall I stop producing my wine

that cheers gods and mortals,

and go to sway over the trees?'

So all the trees said to the bramble,

'You come and reign over us.'

And the bramble said to the trees,

'If in good faith you are anointing me king over you,

then come and take refuge in my shade;

but if not, let fire come out of the bramble

and devour the cedars of Lebanon.'

Judges 9.8-15

CONTENTS

PREFACE

There are many people to thank for helping make this book happen. Kathryn Pritchard at Church House Publishing has, as ever, been a constant source of encouragement and common sense. But I wish to thank all the team at Church House Publishing for their commitment to this project. They are great to work with.

A chat over a cup of coffee with my elder brother, David, confirmed me in a few hunches, helped rectify a few mistakes and make good a few omissions. He probably won't remember the conversation, but I asked him what he thought made a good leader and the few things he said off the cuff, and from a very different experience of leadership, were most useful in the final edit of this book. Paul Bayes also added some extremely helpful comments.

Some of the material was road tested on a headteachers' conference in Oxford, a clergy chapter in Abingdon and a meeting of all the chairs of diocesan synods at their annual gathering in Launde Abbey.

Most of this book draws on the good leadership I have experienced from passionate and committed people over many, many years. In particular, I remember and give thanks for the lives of certain schoolteachers and clergy who have led and cajoled me, helped bring out the best in me, and showed me how to lead others. In particular, I would like to name Robert Warren, James Lawrence, Richard Giles, Eric Kemp, Nigel McCulloch and David Hope. But of course I am still learning. That is one of the main messages of this book: the good leader never stops being a good follower.

Most recently, in the Oxford Diocese, I have been helped enormously by our *Developing Servant Leadership* programme. This has required me to think deeply about my own leadership, about how we share leadership with others and how we train people to lead well. I particularly thank Keith Lamdin for his part in this programme: some of the thinking in this book has been shaped by his creativity and encouragement.

Finally, like all authors of books that appear to tell others what to do, I must publish a disclaimer: I do not practise what I preach with nearly as much integrity as I would wish. Those who know me will know my failings. But I do try to be a learner, and in this way I aspire to be an effective leader. Here are some of the fruits of my learning, which I hope will encourage others. They flow from the wisdom of the Christian tradition. But I dare to think they are relevant for everyone. Our world needs good leadership.

Stephen Cottrell

Bishop of Reading

INTRODUCTION

This is a book about leadership. It is written from a Christian perspective with Christian leaders in mind. But it is also written out of the conviction that the Christian faith and Christian perspectives on leadership have much to offer everyone. For whoever we are, and whatever our responsibilities, all of us exercise leadership somewhere in our lives. It might be that we coach a local football team, or run a choir, or head up a large multinational company, or it might be something really important, such as a family. Often we exercise leadership in several different areas at once. And often that leadership is shared. But to one degree or another we are all leaders.

A lot of popular thinking about leadership, however, seems to suggest that the leader is a single figure, an isolated figure, a lonely figure: someone at the top and leading from the front. This book suggests that there are other ways of leading (from the back or in the middle, for instance) and also dares to propose that the world hasn't necessarily got all the answers. There is some ancient wisdom in the Christian tradition that the Church needs to rediscover and that the world could benefit from learning.

Because I am a bishop in the Church of England, most of the examples I use will inevitably be from the life of the Church and I suppose my primary audience is clergy and other Church leaders. But I am also a parent, working with my wife to lead a family, and there are other areas in my life where I am called to exercise leadership (I am a school governor, for instance). I therefore hope that as well as being a timely antidote to all the self-help, quick-fix, make-do-and-mend, management-style leadership books many of us are heartily fed up with, this book will playfully suggest some other models of leadership that can be of benefit whether or not we reckon we are Christians.

It is a little book. I don't pretend to have all the answers. I've probably only noticed a few of the questions. But because it is a book that says that contemplation is the first mark of leadership, it is a book to be read slowly. You could easily read it all at one go. It is probably better to take it a bit at a time and reflect on what it says to your leadership.

Finally, a disclaimer: although I passionately believe that contemplation and stillness are at the heart of all good leadership, and especially leadership in the Church, I'd be sorry if anyone reading this book thought I was against good practice in management. On the contrary, I believe that good administration and clear purposes and priorities are vital, actually freeing up time for other things, be it the dreaming of new dreams or just having some well-deserved time off.

chapter 1

JUMPING OFF THE BANDWAGON

Sometimes there is a way that seems to be right,
but in the end it is the way to death.

Proverbs 16.25

When I was about twelve years old, I witnessed a frightening accident. A friend of mine fell about 20 feet from a makeshift trapeze: he lay motionless on the ground, his limbs splayed awkwardly around him. We thought he was dead. He was definitely unconscious.

Seized with panic and shock we ran towards the scene of the accident, but we didn't know what to do. We were at Scout camp and someone raced to get the Scoutmaster, who made his way towards the scene. But he didn't run. He didn't seem to realize it was an emergency. And this made us cross. His whole attitude appeared casual, undramatic. He just walked purposefully towards the fallen boy. Afterwards he told us why – it was a first lesson in a different sort of leadership. He told us that he'd needed a few moments to think; he'd needed time to weigh up the situation because his first action had to be the right one. If the fall turned out to be as bad as he feared, there might be no opportunity for a second action. He had also walked so that he wouldn't be out of breath if he needed to give the fallen boy mouth to mouth resuscitation. Actually, this was precisely what was needed. The boy was saved.

You see, it is not always best to be in a hurry.

Sometimes the best leadership requires stillness and composure. Then the right decisions are taken. Then the difficult decisions are faced.

In Peter Weir's film, *Gallipoli*, there is a powerful scene depicting events on the night before thousands of young Australian soldiers are to be sent over the top, where many of them will face certain death. The officer who is in charge at the front line, and who will himself have to lead the assault, sits in his office, not much more than a hollow carved out of the mud, and on a wind-up gramophone listens to a piece of music. Nothing more is said. The camera just lingers on his face. We see him listening intently to the music. We are invited to read his thoughts. For a few moments we get inside what it must be like, not just to be involved in that sort of situation, but to lead others through it.

It's years since I've seen the film, and I can't remember what the music was – I think it was a piece of opera – but in my mind I see him sitting there, contemplating the music, weighing up what lay ahead of him, connecting himself with something beautiful that was beyond and away from the horrors of the First World War.

I suppose you could view this as escapism, as a way of avoiding reality, but I read the scene differently. Here is a man in a position of terrible responsibility, following orders, but at the same time having to deliver costly orders to others. He sees the madness of it; he feels and holds the pain of it; is trapped and constrained by the choices that others have made. He knows what he has to do, but still looks beyond it. Amid the frightful inhumanity and degradation of trench warfare he connects himself to a beauty that must seem unreachable and yet at the same time is one of the few things worth seeking. In those few moments of contemplation he is able to compose himself and discover within himself the resources he needs to lead his men. What we see is not the leadership itself, but a man discovering resources to lead by retreating to a place of stillness and contemplation. In the midst of the horror, he stops, and in stopping is better able to carry out the responsibilities of his leadership. He is drawing on resources outside himself.

And now I am reminded of other leaders who not only steered the ship more effectively because they had dared to stop and test the direction of the tide, but were also able to remind themselves of the bigger picture and be more creative in their leadership. They allowed their leadership to be led.

It is said that during difficult meetings that ran late into the evening Abraham Lincoln led his cabinet colleagues outside and bid them contemplate the night sky for a few minutes. He would then share with them his knowledge of the make up of the galaxies, reckoning that when they were all put in touch with something beyond themselves, they would be better able to deal with the business in front of them.

In the New Testament we often find Jesus taking himself off on his own, away from the crowds and their competing expectations. Here, in sometimes painful solitude, he would think and pray and contemplate. And from the well of this contemplation his leadership would be drawn.

Whatever sort of leadership we exercise, indeed, whether or not we think of ourselves as leaders, time spent in reflective attentiveness, what the Church calls contemplation, makes for healthier and more fruitful living. But I say this against the backdrop of a world of remorseless and implacable busyness. We seem hell bent on filling every waking moment – and most of the sleeping ones as well – with noise and activity. Time for reflection is squeezed out. In fact sleeping moments are harder to come by. We sleep less than we did 40 years ago. We work longer hours. And we are constantly chided and chivvied by the chatter of the TV, the chirping of the mobile phone and the clamour of email. We are tied to the trees but more and more cut off from the wood.

The assumption of our society is that bigger and faster equals better and more efficient.

But I want to question that assumption.

I want to dream a different way of leading, and my first point is this: creativity is usually cultivated in the soil of contemplation. The ability to act decisively (and correctly!) often arises from a well of stillness. The best things in life, from a bottle of Châteauneuf-du-Pape to the ability to play Beethoven's *Diabelli Variations*, take time. Hence I am suggesting that stopping and thinking and being still should be the first requirement of creative leadership: a better way of doing it; a way that flows from the Christian tradition, but also a way that is relevant for any sort of leadership.

I plan to upend some commonly held assumptions and garner fresh perspective from some of those hoary old truisms that most of us take as given.

Most of all I want to help us step off the bandwagon that assumes that the world in all its busyness has all the answers on this question of leadership.

I also write this out of an abiding belief in the benefits and delights of the shallow end. Those same people who drive the bandwagon and who – as we shall see – tell us to hit the ground running are the ones who also tell us to jump in at the deep end. Well, despite the macho posturing, do you know anyone who actually learned to swim in the deep end? I don't. Though I've heard of one or two people who drowned that way.

Most of us learned to swim in the shallow end. We weren't out of our depth. We were cheered on by encouraging parents. We were kept afloat by arm bands. Our feet touched the ground. We were painstakingly put through our paces by a patient swimming instructor who knew how to balance carefully the security of knowing we were safe – despite appearances, this water would hold us – with the stretching challenge of danger. We inched our way into the deep. We slowly learned to swim.

This is how most important things are learned.

Slowly.

With instruction.

When I learned to ride a bike, I started off with stabilizers. Even then I fell off many times before I discovered the astonishing truth that the faster I pedalled the better I stayed on. When I learned to play the piano, I began with just the right hand, and with each finger placed over a single key, and it was weeks before I knew any tune with more than five notes.

When I learned to exercise leadership in the Church, I received training; I worked with a more experienced priest; I was led into taking and understanding responsibility and valuing the contribution of others. I also had to unlearn all those half truths that are so often bandied about and that this book seeks to debunk.

The received wisdom of the world is that you make 'your' mark. This book is about 'our' mark. The world says, 'Don't state the obvious.' But I reckon that articulating the vision and reminding people of what is fundamental are the first requirements of leadership. The world says, 'Don't reinvent the wheel.' But other people's wheels don't always fit. The world says, 'Don't count your chickens before they hatch.' But we need a big vision to counter the prevalent and all-consuming cynicism that is eating up our culture.

The world says you need a thick skin. But most of us are born with hearts that break. We need to learn to exercise leadership without pretending we can't be hurt. Otherwise we really will be heading for a breakdown. And there is more besides. From the perspective of the shallow end we can view leadership differently.

Finally – the idea behind the title of this book – we don't need to hit the ground running. There is another way. And it is this, more than anything else, that unlocks a different way of leading, a way that is deeply rooted in the Christian tradition and a way that is relevant and helpful to all people exercising leadership whether or not they are Christians. Irritatingly, it is a way that the Christian Church seems often to have forgotten. But it is a way of leading that this book aims to rehabilitate. So let's look at this in a bit more detail.

Listening

What is the key skill needed for the sort of leadership we are exploring in this book? I think it is listening. More than anything else the wise leader, the leader who values the contributions of others and is prepared to let things happen at the right pace, is someone who dares to listen. This is the reason for stopping. We need to take stock. We need to weigh the options. We need to heed advice. We need to understand the complexity. Only good listening can achieve this. And good listening takes time.

In the New Testament, Jesus models for us what a good listener is like. It is remarkable how in nearly every situation in which Jesus engages with people we find him listening before he speaks. One of the best examples is the conversation on the Emmaus Road on the first Easter day. Jesus has appeared to two of his disciples but they haven't recognized him, so he says to them: 'What are you discussing with each other while you walk along?' (Luke 24.17). His attitude is one of open vulnerability. He allows the conversation to be led by their agenda. It is not that he doesn't have anything to say, only that he knows that his words will lack clarity and precision if they don't speak directly to the needs and questions of the people he is with.

Leaders need this same attitude. Listening is good in itself. It is very important that leaders demonstrate their care and concern for those around them. But listening is also the best way of discovering the best solutions. As any doctor will tell you, without a diagnosis there can never be a cure. Hence when you visit the doctor, you are the person to speak first. You describe your symptoms and your doctor listens carefully, probing you with questions, seeking to discover the precise nature of the problem. Only after that does your doctor offer a possible cure and even then a process of dialogue usually continues.

Leaders do the same. If we have assumed the answer before ever really diagnosing the problem, we will not only belittle and alienate those around us who are seeing it differently, we will fail. Wise leaders will be good listeners, always listening carefully to the challenges of the situation they are in, and also to the views, advice and experience of those they are working with.

There is also another sort of listening that arises directly out of a spirit of contemplation. It is about listening to the signs of the times, being in tune with what is happening in contemporary culture and in the world. And also listening to your own self. Christians will of course speak about listening to God, too, but whether or not you believe in God, I want to direct you to that way of listening that is about perception and instinct, where we catch hold of a mood, or lay claim to a deep-seated conviction, or yield ourselves to a new insight. Listening carefully to these inner and outer voices can transform the way we view a situation. They generate creative dialogue.

The Christian writer Henri Nouwen has said this:

> It is not enough for the priests and ministers of
> the future to be moral people, well trained, eager
> to help their fellow humans, and able to respond
> creatively to the burning issues of their time. All
> of that is very valuable and important, but it is
> not the heart of Christian leadership. The central
> question is, are the leaders of the future truly
> men and women of God, people with an ardent
> desire to dwell in God's presence, to listen to
> God's voice, to look upon God's beauty, to touch
> God's incarnate Word and to taste fully God's
> infinite goodness? . . . Their leadership must be
> rooted in the permanent, intimate relationship
> with the incarnate Word, Jesus, and they need
> to find there the source for their words, advice
> and guidance. Through the discipline of
> contemplative prayer, Christian leaders have to
> learn to listen again and again to the voice of
> love and to find there the wisdom and courage
> to address whatever issue presents itself to them.[1]

[1] Henri J. M. Nouwen, *In the Name of Jesus: Reflections on Christian Leadership*, Darton, Longman & Todd, 1989, pp. 29–31.

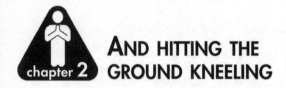

AND HITTING THE GROUND KNEELING

chapter 2

> The plans of the diligent lead surely to abundance,
> but everyone who is hasty comes only to want.
>
> Proverbs 21.5

I had my eureka moment about two years ago in the middle of a meeting to shortlist applicants for a vacancy in a parish that had better remain nameless. Eight or nine people had applied and we were carefully considering them in turn, sorting our papers into piles of 'definitely yes', 'maybe', 'no' and 'not until hell freezes over'. We reached a bit of an impasse over one candidate who had lots to offer but didn't particularly fit the profile and person specification we had before us.

'What we need', said one of my fellow shortlisters, 'is someone who can hit the ground running.'

I had heard this phrase hundreds of times before, but I suddenly found myself wanting to scream out that this was precisely what we didn't need. Not just in this job, but in almost every job, or at least in virtually every job except those actually quite rare situations where things are so dire that only someone coming in and acting very swiftly will save the day. So, yes, I want a lifeguard who can hit the ground running. I want a paramedic who can hit the ground running. If I'm drowning, I don't want someone who will wait on the beach weighing up the options. I want someone who will jump in and save me. If I've been run over by a bus, I don't want someone who will keep to the speed limit and take half an hour to get to me. I want the siren blaring and the blue light flashing and the ambulance with me in five minutes. But in most other leadership situations – indeed, remembering the crucial patience of that Scoutmaster, even for the lifeguard, who needs to check the currents and the wind direction so he doesn't end up drowning himself as well, even for the paramedic who, if she does recklessly drive through all the red lights, will get someone else run over – a more reflective and collaborative approach to leadership is much more useful.

The ability to hit the ground running may appear to be an attractive quality to seek out in a new leader, and of course it is important in the sense of finding a candidate with relevant experience who can therefore offer some assurance of actually being able to do the job in question. But I sense that something else is going on when people make such a big deal of this particular quality. Is the desire to have someone who can hit the ground running also a desire to have someone who will be busy; someone who will take charge in a way that will leave everyone else free to abdicate, or at least back-pedal on their own responsibilities? Is it just another way of buying into the all-pervading busyness that we find everywhere else in life? Because while it is good to have a leader with experience, doesn't experience sometimes teach us that rushing at things is not the best way to proceed?

When someone hits the ground running, there is all the superficial attraction of movement and progress. But there is no guarantee that they are going in the right direction. The first mark of leadership that we can discern from the Christian perspective is this: find time to stop. The leader is sometimes the person who dares to do nothing; the person who is prepared to be a still point of reflective consideration when everyone else is just busy; the person who carefully and prayerfully weighs up options, seeks consensus, builds coalitions, really maps out the ground, before making the crucially important, but fearsomely difficult, decision of discerning which direction should be taken. It occurred to me that the person who has dared to stop might also be the person who, where necessary, is prepared to make the bold and costly decision of swimming against the current.

And in a healthy organization, be it a family or a multinational company, these sorts of decision – the really big ones – should never be left to one person. The really wise leader will at this point allow herself to be led: by instinct; by collaboration; by listening to the wisdom and experience of others; and by a painstaking discernment of the choices that lie ahead. The responsibility will, ultimately, rest with the leader. But he will, from the start, have shown himself to be someone who prizes collaboration, who values working with others and who considers contemplation to be leadership's most vital task.

Take the well-worn example of moving to a new house with a new and unknown garden: only if you are foolish will you rush in to dig up the beds in early spring before seeing what the garden will bring forth of itself. Why? Because ninety-nine times out of a hundred there was another gardener here before you. You are receiving the baton – or in this case the trowel – from your predecessor; and while you must lead in the way you discern to be necessary, the day will come when you too must move on. So the wise leader waits and looks. What has already been planted? Where and when will it bloom and how will it bear fruit? It really takes a whole year of tending carefully what you have received (and not making any changes at all) before you can begin to see what might usefully be done next. Even then, you are wonderfully aware that you are building on another person's work.

The idea of the leader as the pioneering individual is dangerously mistaken in almost every situation except those rare circumstances when you really are in a completely new situation. Since there is nothing new under the sun, it is much better to assume that your predecessor was not the fool you are presuming him to be and that, in fact, you have much to learn from observing the contours and the patterns of his work. Even in parenthood, when you will inevitably be the first parent to the child you have conceived, and you are famously doing the most important job of your life and the one with the least preparation or training, there are still countless other parents who have gone before you and therefore much wisdom to be gained. There is the model of your own parents, and even if we side with Larkin and believe that all parents mess up their offspring one generation after another, there is another lesson to be learned here: learning from the ones who are led. This is one of the key lessons to be learned from parenting, a lesson that, it seems to me, has the potential to shape our entire leadership: as a mother bonds with a child, it is as much the child teaching the woman to be a mother as the mother leading the child.

This insight underpins some of the most radical teaching that you will find in the New Testament. When asked by his followers who will be greatest in the kingdom of God, Jesus places a little child in their midst: unless you receive the kingdom as a child, he says, you cannot enter it. This was both a shock and a rebuke to the disciples. You see, what they were after was not the sort of sacrificial, servant leadership that is modelled by Jesus; what they wanted was power.

The person who hits the ground running is often a person running away from their predecessor. When I have heard clergy talking about their work in a parish, I'm afraid to say that I've often heard them saying that things seem to have turned around in the last three years, or four years, or since a certain date. When I quiz them about what it is that has happened since that date, or what was the turning point three years ago, I usually discover that this marked their arrival in the parish. Although they are not consciously rubbishing what went before, that is the effect of their words. It is a depressingly familiar scenario: leaders rushing into new situations without daring to stop and look around first. It is also symptomatic of a desire for power, summed up in that other familiar phrase that fills me with dread, 'I need to make my mark.' Or, even worse, 'I need to make my mark in the first year, or else it will be too late.'

The object of leadership is not to make a mark; at least, not in this way. A Chinese proverb observes that when the greatest leaders have done their work, the people say, 'We did it ourselves.' Let us, right near the beginning of this book, nail a key issue for everything else that follows by asking: What is the aim of leadership? Well, once again, it doesn't matter what you are leading – you might be responsible for laying on a meal for twenty unexpected family guests with only your three recalcitrant and inexperienced teenage children and their friend from next door to help you; you might be a Girl Guide leader, play-group supervisor or community police officer, or you might have just landed the job as CEO of GlaxoSmithKline – your task as leader is the same. Your job is to enable others to do their very best and to achieve their fullest potential, and for the purpose of your organization – whatever it is – to be advanced. It is not you the leader who has to make a mark, but the work you are undertaking and the people you are working with. Together you seek to achieve the very best that you can. To lead a corporate effort, with a clear sense of the direction that should be taken, and with a determination to bring out the best from all those who are working with you, that is your goal.

Again, parenting provides the key. The successful parent is the one who enables the child to grow and leave. A successful home is one that is left behind. If your child is still living with you in his mid fifties, this is not success: he may still love you, and you him, but if that love has not enabled him to become his own independent person, if it has stifled him and held him back, then it has turned out not to be love at all, but, rather, a smothering obsessive inability to let him become the person he was meant to be. Potential has been limited and curtailed rather than advanced and extended.

Therefore real leadership must, at every turn, take the risk of allowing others to make mistakes as they learn their place within the whole. Just as the good parent provides the scaffolding which, when the child's life is built, is removed and never needed again, so the good leader is doing the same: building a framework within which others will thrive and the enterprise of the company or association prosper.

Success is not the aim. Sometimes we will not even know what success looks like (this is often the case in the work of a community like the Church). Sometimes there must be the refining fire of what looks like failure. As the parent allows the child to grow, so there must be the setbacks and disasters that contribute to maturity. Hence the mature leader, the best leader, is by nature reflective. Leaders will not need to rush in. They will not need to instantly make their mark. They will prefer to see their mark in the lives of others who are not clones of themselves but people growing into the rich diversity of their potential. They will not clamour for instant approval, quick fixes, or be over worried by the latest poll ratings. They will not paper over the cracks of the challenges they encounter, nor dig up the work of their predecessors before they have allowed it to bear fruit. And if this sort of reflective leadership does not come naturally, then the example of Jesus is inspiring and gives practical help. Again and again in the Gospels, Jesus withdraws from the company of his followers. He goes to a lonely place and he spends time alone in prayer.

There is a wonderfully comic moment near the beginning of Mark's Gospel, which makes this point well. It is before dawn and Jesus has taken himself off to a deserted place to pray. The disciples hunt him down and tell him that everybody is searching for him. Jesus snubs them: 'Let us go on to the neighbouring towns,' he replies (Mark 1.37-38)! In other words, he deliberately turns his back on the crowd and all their expectations. He turns away from the easy popularity that is on offer. He pointedly fails to meet the demands of the disciples and all those others who want his attention. His behaviour is characterized by an evident lack of availability that is at odds with a certain feverish desire to be always available that is the all too prevalent hallmark of certain types of leadership. Why? Because he has a higher agenda, one that is not about making that sort of mark.

Being available must never be the defining characteristic of effective leadership. After all, as soon as you have made a commitment to be available to one person you have by definition made yourself unavailable to everyone else. Having not mastered the art of bi-location, all of us are bound by the laws of physics – even Jesus during his ministry on earth – and can only be in one place at a time. The wise leader will therefore make wise choices about how time is managed, giving first priority to that space for refreshment and discernment where decisions about the right use of the *rest* of the time can be profitably made.

This also helps avoid the pitfall of co-dependency. We rush around saying yes to everything and dancing to other people's tunes because we want their approval. All of us have locked ourselves into patterns of working that feed off one other and lead nowhere. Too many leaders have indeed hit the ground running, but as well as having no idea whether or not they are going in the right direction, having failed to stop and discern what might be the right way forward, they are also allowing themselves to be driven by the agendas of others, all in a vain, though often subconscious, attempt to court a popularity that can never be achieved since the culture itself is so frantic that everyone is suggesting a different direction anyway!

By stopping, by making himself unavailable to anyone except himself and, in his case, God, Jesus models a different sort of leadership, one that is relevant to all of us whether or not we believe in God. This is what I meant when I referred to the 'higher agenda' of Jesus. He makes himself available to the sort of reflective consideration that gives time to discerning *purpose* and *direction*. Then, when he does move forward, it is with confidence and clarity.

To do this takes courage: the disciples wanted Jesus somewhere else, and there was a large crowd of people with all sorts of needs that required attention. And it is not that these needs were not important. They probably were. It is just that they were not *most* important.

In so much leadership the greatest enemy of the best is the second best. We settle down to satisfy the perfectly good and honourable requests and demands of everyone else but never get round to discerning our primary calling. Dare to hit the ground kneeling and another way of leadership opens up.

Affirmation

Jesus' ministry began in the wilderness. We are told that as soon as he is baptized in the River Jordan he is driven into the desert. For Jesus, this desert experience is not one of quiet reflection or rest, but a place of testing. Jesus seeks to discover what his vocation might be. He tests out what direction his life must take. He wrestles with himself as much as with God. Then after forty days the devil appears to him and he faces three particular temptations.

First of all, Jesus is tempted to turn stones into bread. This is a temptation to be flashy, to be relevant.

The second temptation is to throw himself from the roof of the Temple and let angels catch him in their arms. This is a temptation to be spectacular, to be popular.

The third temptation – the most dangerous and seductive of all – is to be powerful. The devil shows Jesus all the kingdoms of the world and promises they will be his if he bows down and worships him.

These temptations are alive in all of us. They can easily lure us away from the goals we are aiming for. Regularly stepping off the treadmill will help. Instead of being flashy, we need to allow ourselves to be drawn back to the vision that inspired us in the first place. Instead of seeking popularity and other people's adulation, we need to ensure that we get our affirmation from our faithfulness to this vision. Instead of looking for power, we must aspire to be servants of the vision, sharing responsibility and leadership and building up the gifts of others.

The temptations don't go away. And of course we will often go wrong. But a discipline of separation will not only keep us in touch with what we are calling in this book the higher agenda, it will remind us of our first love, and enable us to overcome fear and find real affirmation.

For Jesus, this affirmation, which is the wellspring of his ministry, comes in a single defining moment, the effects of which are felt for the rest of his life. As he surfaces out of the waters of baptism, he hears a voice from heaven say, 'You are my Son, the Beloved; with you I am well pleased' (Mark 1.11).

Very few of us will ever have such a clear sense of God's affirmation and blessing. Many of us, however, will have foundations in our lives through the love and stability we have experienced from parents, siblings and friends. I particularly remember the affirmation I received from my parents, and also from teachers who continued to believe in me and support me when I was struggling academically. However, and this is another vitally important point for leadership from a Christian perspective, *even if we haven't*, this affirmation is available to us and can be found through making ourselves available to the presence of God. Indeed, for those of us who are leading a Christian organization of any sort, it is precisely this wellspring of affirmation – often best accessed through stillness and contemplation – that is the most attractive thing we have to offer. Strange, then, that we often seem to act as if the only way we can make ourselves attractive to the world is by being as frantic as everyone else!

The Christian leader – whatever the organization – can be the still point at the centre of the maelstrom, the one whose judgement can be trusted, the one who is not seeking her own ends or his own self-advancement, but cares for those in their charge. Such leaders have an inner security and peace that is both a gift from God and the most important gift they can bestow on others: they are leaders who allow themselves to be led.

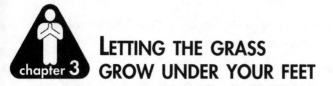

chapter 3

LETTING THE GRASS GROW UNDER YOUR FEET

> One who spares words is knowledgeable; one who is
> cool in spirit has understanding.
>
> Proverbs 17.27

So how does this contemplative approach to leadership work out
in practise and how does it bear fruit? What happens when we let
the grass grow under our feet for once and just spend a bit of time
looking around without imagining that we've got all the answers
and that no one before us had anything much to offer?

As a Christian leader, I cannot conceive of doing my job without
ensuring that my first priority is time apart and time alone. For me,
this manifests itself in two particular ways. The first is prayer. This
is how my day begins. I follow a pattern of prayer that is set out by
the Church of England and is part of a tradition that goes back
centuries, a way of praise and reflection that has been shaped by
the experience of countless millions of Christians. It is a way that
works for me, though it is not without its struggle. (There are
always pressing voices inside me beckoning me to get on with a
piece of correspondence or some other apparently urgent matter.)
A discipline as well as a desire is required to create space where
'doing nothing' (at least as the world would understand it) takes
priority. For me, it is helpful to have someone alongside me to share

this space and to pray with me, though this is not always possible and for some people may never be.

Into this carved-out space of contemplation I not only have the opportunity to reflect on the wisdom and insights of Christian scripture – the set readings and prayers that I follow – but I can bring to mind the concerns of the day, intentionally laying before God the people and situations I know I will be facing. There is also an opportunity for conscious thanksgiving, which is a marvellous antidote to the world-weary cynicism that so often kicks about in our heads (and all too often finds its way on to our tongues). And there is adoration, that ancient Christian discipline of prayer where we don't really do or say anything but simply enjoy the company of God and experience God's love for what it is, the precious gift of presence.

The wonderful thing about this sort of prayer is that it is gloriously affirming; I rest in the presence of God and know myself to be a precious part of God's creation, but not its centre. As we have already noted, many leaders rush around doing lots of things because they are seeking affirmation in the wrong place, trying to keep everyone happy rather then being engaged in the more noble vocation of making them holy, helping them become themselves.

On a very practical level, this sort of prayer is also useful when you face a particularly sticky situation or a really challenging person: there is nothing like a little bit of praise and thanksgiving to help unlock a stalemate. It is so easy to pigeonhole a difficult person as a problem rather than seeing their goodness, their talents, their dreams and, quite possibly, the way you are a problem to them! Pausing to give thanks for that person, praising them for who they are, despite the fact that they are making your life difficult, changes attitudes and releases energy. Consequently, positive outcomes are much more likely to emerge. Conflict gives way to consensus.

There are plenty of books and resources available to help Christian people get into this sort of daily discipline of prayer. Other religious traditions will have their own resources. But my point in this book is more basic: whether or not you think of yourself as religious, this way of beginning the day, this spiritual discipline, is good for you. Space away from the usual routines of work and leisure allows a kind of settling of the mind to take place: priorities are sorted, concerns are placed in a wider perspective, and progress (or the lack of it) is discerned. You find it is possible to create a kind of distance that enables you to see the wood as well as the trees. You are able to be thankful and to consciously identify what the day holds and how it can be faced.

And you can do all this without calling it prayer – it can just be space to ponder and reflect – but obviously I write this believing that it opens up a whole new dimension of possibilities where we can actually receive affirmation from a power and a source of goodness much greater than ourselves. This, more than anything, puts the whole of our lives and all we are doing into right perspective. For I am not the centre of the universe and the well-being of the universe does not depend on me. I have my part to play and I can lead others to understand their place within the whole. It also means that our thanksgivings are not merely offered silently to ourselves, but to a God who is really capable of listening and rejoicing with us. It acknowledges that there is wisdom to the universe, which we can access and which can shape our values, priorities and decision-making.

All this is commonplace within the Christian tradition and within all the great religious traditions of the world. I am suggesting it is a way of exercising leadership that can be of enormous practical value to everyone.

The second thing I regularly do is go away for a day every month. I used to call this a 'prayer day', but the truth is that I don't necessarily do much praying. I have come to understand these days as 'reconnecting with the vision' days; times when I can get some distance from the unrelenting demands of the immediate and focus on the important. I go somewhere where I can get away from the phone. This usually means a retreat house, but I suppose it could be anywhere. I usually start off just by enjoying reading the newspaper all the way through. I then might go for a walk. I will usually have a good long snooze after lunch. Sometimes I will jot down a few thoughts in the afternoon.

The effect of the day is that I return home not only rested and refreshed, but also refocused. I can see again what I am about. I have fresh clarity about what I'm trying to achieve and what my priorities should be. I am put back in touch with the higher agenda. And in order to do this I don't actually need much more than space and time. But of course these are usually the things that are in shortest supply.

Another way of understanding what happens on these days is in terms of what I wish to call 'first love'. Most of us are engaged in leadership because we have a passion and a desire for the organization we are leading. This is how we got into it in the first place and now we have risen to a point where we have responsibility for shaping its life and future. This passion that got us involved is our first love. But sometimes the pressures and demands of keeping the show on the road mean that we lose our first love, we forget why we started, we become weary and cynical. Tasks become ends in themselves rather than steps towards the goals and desires that used to motivate us.

Reclaiming this first love can be one of the best ways of renewing our energy for leadership. In other words, we are not just inspired by what we see as the end, or the goal, of our enterprise, but we can also be equally inspired by our beginnings. A day away, as I am describing it, is different from a day of planning for the future. This is also a good thing to do, but is usually better done alongside colleagues, where shared vision for the future can be nurtured. A regular day *on your own* can be a way of getting back in touch with first love.

To this end I am always particularly moved by a passage in the Bible from the book of Revelation, the last book in the New Testament. The writer, John, has a vision of seven golden lampstands, each representing a Christian community. God speaks of his concerns for each community. To the church in Ephesus John is told to write this:

> I know your works, your toil and your patient endurance
> . . . I also know that you are enduring patiently and
> bearing up for the sake of my name, and that you have
> not grown weary. But I have this against you, that you
> have abandoned the love you had at first. Remember

> then from what you have fallen; repent, and do the
> works you did at first.
>
> Revelation 2.2-5

Whenever I read these words I feel as if they are addressed to me. For I know that I do work hard. I know that I endure and sometimes I even do it patiently! But the real complaint is this: 'You have abandoned the love you had at first.' It is returning to this love that will be the seedbed for renewal and change in the future. And all I need to do is find the time to remember.

So if you are finding it fearsomely difficult to manage, let alone love, that difficult teenager who has suddenly hurled himself into your life, remember the little child you first held. And although you will have to love him differently today, make sure it is the same love that is being offered. And if the small business you have carefully grown over many years has become burdensome with all the additional responsibilities of personnel management, health and safety regulations, risk assessments, equal opportunities and VAT receipts, remember the thrill of your first sale, remember the good that is brought to the lives of others because you are an employer and see the bigger picture of what you do. And if you are a priest, and prayer has become a professional activity, something you do for others in church but rarely find time for on your own, remember the first time you celebrated Holy Communion, remember standing at the altar and holding bread and wine and saying the words that Jesus said, and remember sharing that bread and wine with all those people who also come to God with their brokenness and longing, and see that the daily round of your faithfulness in serving others is a participation in God's great offering of himself in Jesus Christ.

The other thing that emerges from time consciously given to reflection and contemplation is creativity. Not only do I learn to appreciate the creativity and wisdom of what has gone before – I see the garden growing – but often the best ideas and the most creative thinking emerge from the attentive idleness that a day of resting and dreaming encourages. Having stepped back from the fray, having resisted the temptation to rush in and change everything quickly, or to set a new course without being sure where to go, I am able to see more clearly how this enterprise I am leading can be enhanced, until that day when I pass it on to someone else.

So the advice of this book so far and all that follows is to hit the ground kneeling. In order to exercise any kind of fruitful, transforming and enabling leadership, the first foundation stone we lay must be space and time. If we rush at leadership we may well make the wrong choices. Two years down the road we will either be burnt out with exhaustion, stretched out by other people's agendas, or wrung out because of a lack of vision or direction.

Sharpening the saw

The lifestyle guru Stephen Covey tells the instructive story of two men sawing wood. One person works solidly through the day. The other takes a break for ten minutes every hour. At the end of the day the person who has taken the breaks has cut considerably more wood.

'How can this be?' asks the other man.

'Every time I took a break', comes the reply, 'I sharpened my saw.'

Rest and contemplation have several interrelated benefits for all work and especially for leadership. They

- put us back in touch with the big picture;

- put us back in touch with first love;

- help us reset the compass;

- provide much-needed balance;

- provide physical rest and opportunity for recreation;

- and as this story illustrates, provide opportunity for training and retraining, thus improving efficiency and output.

chapter 4

STATING THE OBVIOUS

Keep straight the path of your feet, and all your ways
will be sure.

Proverbs 4.26

Do you remember the story of the emperor's new clothes? Feeding
his vanity, the designers of his non-existent clothes find him easy
to deceive. And whether from fear of the king, or just the plain
ordinary fear of looking stupid, everyone else plays along, not one
of them wanting to step out from the crowd. Only the little boy has
the courage to state the obvious – the king is naked!

Often the leader is called to play the same part. It is not necessarily
the dazzlingly brilliant insight that marks out the best leaders, but
the ability to do the very thing that so many people wearily tell us
we mustn't do: state the obvious.

Now of course it is highly desirable that the leader should have the
odd dazzlingly brilliant insight, but the more important quality in
terms of day-to-day leadership is the willingness to recall the
organization to its primary vocation.

When I became priest in charge of St Wilfrid's, a church on a
small council estate to the west of Chichester, I was astonished to
discover that the church did not have a noticeboard or a font. The
plot quickly thickened when I discovered that no one seemed
particularly perturbed by their absence. These two rather glaring

omissions told an eloquent tale about the health of the church I was being called to lead. The commonly held view seemed to be this: Why would we need a noticeboard? We know what time the service starts. Why would we need a font? We're all baptized.

Of course, no one actually put it like this; but behind the prevarications and excuses lay an attitude that revealed that this church, though full of kind and generous people, had become a sort of club; and it had certainly lost or forgotten its vocation to serve the local community.

A church without a noticeboard or a font is a church serving itself. The missing noticeboard, the absent font, became symbols in my mind of how the church needed to change. And looking back, if I'm honest, I think I probably made the mistake I am urging you to avoid, that of hitting the ground running and doing lots of things to try to hasten change without properly discerning vision and purpose. I do, however, remember getting some things the right way round. Although I was sorely tempted to go out and buy a noticeboard and put it on the wall and have done with it, I remember thinking that it would be much better if the people of the church arrived at this conclusion for themselves and actually wanted to start doing something to publicize their life.

But because there was no font, I was aware that the malaise was quite deep-seated. The font is the place of entry into the Christian community. Without a font, the church had become like a beautiful house with no door. We were already inside, so we didn't need to worry about helping others to join us. We had forgotten that this was one of our primary tasks. What I needed to do was to recall the church to its vocation to be a community that existed for God and for others. But I also realized that that would probably take more than simply telling people what they were supposed to be.

The Americans have a good saying for this – if they ain't heard it, you ain't said it! For communication to take place, for learning to happen, rather more is required than simply telling people what it is you want them to hear. I may have spoken, but there is no guarantee that anyone has heard.

The job of the leader is to find ways of stating the obvious. It is the task of leadership to articulate vision and endlessly recall the community or organization to its fundamental purpose and values. But we don't just do this by talking. Often the communication of vision requires prophetic acts that embody a whole range of ideas and enable people to creatively engage with what is being demonstrated. We need to do something as well as say something. A relatively simple action can speak louder than a thousand words and encompass a whole way of looking at a complexity of related issues.

So I waited for an opportunity to enable the church to discover for itself why a font might be a good idea, why a noticeboard was necessary, and my opportunity came after about six months through the unlikely vehicle of the parish jumble sale.

This church had four jumble sales a year – they were red-letter days in the calendar. Two weeks before the jumble sale the parish would be leafleted telling people that the great day was approaching and asking them to be generous in donating jumble. One week before, volunteers knocked on doors and collected the jumble. On the

Friday evening, a small army of people sorted the jumble into clothes or bric-a-brac or books. Then there was the day itself and even more people were involved – scores of them – eager helpers who didn't usually have anything else to do with the life of the church but were enthusiastically dedicated to the redistribution of jumble. Stalls were set up. Cakes were baked in readiness for weary jumblers to be given post-bargain-hunting recuperation. Someone was posted on the door, which was kept safely locked.

As the hour of the opening approached, people would start to gather, impatiently waiting to be let in and for business to commence. A queue snaked around the corner of the hall that adjoined the church. This was not a predicament we were used to. Crowd control was not one of our problems on a Sunday morning. When the door was opened, a tide of humanity swept into the hall; the weaker brethren were elbowed out of the way and shed-loads of jumble were sifted, sampled, stickled and sold. It was usually all over after about two hours. Everything was cleared up. A man with a van appeared from I don't know where and for a fiver took everything that was left off our hands. The money was counted and we usually did quite well – though with jumble sales, quite well doesn't really amount to that much. We all went home.

Now I don't want to sound snootily superior about all this because in their own strange way these jumble sales provided some sort of service to the community before boot sales and eBay took jumble to a new level. They were good fun. But after I had been through this quarterly cycle twice, I was beginning to get worried about what these jumble sales said about the church. I had faithfully leafleted the homes, collected the jumble, sorted and sold with the best of them. I felt I had done my bit to watch this patch of the garden grow and had seen it for what it was – not wrong in itself, but giving out some unintended messages to the community.

So I came to the PCC – that is, the church council who share responsibility with the priest for leadership and decision-making in the Christian community – cap in hand, and told them I had a bit of an idea and was hoping for their support. I told them that I wanted to cancel the next jumble sale. Not cancel them all. Not cancel them for ever, but just the next one. And in its place I proposed that we do something else. I was concerned that the people of our parish were getting a rather distorted view of what the church was about: I was beginning to fear that they thought the church existed to redistribute their old stuff. After all, we were remarkably committed to it. Four times a year we knocked on their doors and asked them to give us their stuff. Four times a year we invited them to our hall on a Saturday afternoon to buy other people's junk. Perhaps, I suggested, this was what they thought the church was for; that we were a sort of old clothes, bric-a-brac and book redistributor. I said to them that I noticed we had never leafleted the parish or knocked on doors at Christmas inviting people to come to our services. Nor were we planning to do anything like this at Easter. We didn't do anything to encourage people to bring their children for baptism. We didn't provide opportunities for people to come and find out about the Christian faith. We didn't even have a noticeboard on the wall outside saying what time the services were. But we did collect and sell jumble.

So I suggested that instead of another sale we have a church open day, a day when we invited the local community to come to the church, just like they did for a jumble sale, but this time to experience something of why the church was really here.

My idea was greeted with stunned silence – but not opposition. I assured the PCC that the following quarter the jumble sale would go ahead as usual. This was not about the jumble sale, it was about the lack of anything else that might say to the people we were called to serve that we had a purpose beyond our own preservation – for the motivation for the jumble sales, though there were all sorts of other benefits, was survival. Apart from our Sunday services, everything else we did was about raising money. But this left a slightly sour taste of self-preservation in the mouth. We wanted to raise the money, but we weren't necessarily prepared to give much of it ourselves. I don't know about you, but when my gas bill or phone bill lands on the mat, I don't usually decide to pay it by erecting a trestle table on the front drive, piling it high with old junk that I no longer need, and selling it to my neighbours so that they, in effect, end up paying for my heating! No, I budget my income so that there is sufficient to pay for my bills.

The endless cycle of jumble sales, the missing font, the blank wall, revealed a malaise. We had forgotten why we existed. We knew it had to be paid for – we had to keep the show on the road somehow – but we had little sense that the church belonged to us, that this was an organization and community that we were so committed to that we were prepared to pay for it. We thought the bills were someone else's, and so we expected someone else to pay.

All I did at that PCC meeting was state the obvious. (And it helps, on such occasions, to do it with a smile and with a lightness of touch, for these were good people doing their very best.) What had been lacking was leadership. Not leadership that would browbeat them into a change of direction that made no sense, but leadership that would enable them to own the organization for themselves and together discern the right way forward; leadership that took a few steps forward, to show people where we could be going, but then came back to join them and, leading from the middle, encourage them to get out map and compass.

So, as a step along this road, I suggested an open day. Nothing else, but a first step on a potential different journey. And there and then, in the same meeting, I asked everyone to write down two or three things that they thought were absolutely essential to the life of the church, the real reason why we existed. And what was enormously encouraging was that it didn't take long for people to find things they could say, things that really mattered to them. And just as encouraging, there was a clear consensus.

Funnily enough, it wasn't quite as easy to get church members to volunteer to knock on doors inviting people to come to a church open day as it had been to get them to knock on doors to collect jumble! But the open day did go ahead. And people did come. And we did find ways of presenting to the community some of the basic points about why the church exists. In due course, not only did we have a noticeboard, but the bills were paid and everything that we made from future jumble sales was given back to the community in charitable service.

So, then, one of the primary roles of leadership is to articulate the vision of the organization. Sometimes this vision will emerge through contemplation. Sometimes it will take shape through conversation. But in both cases the job of the leader is to recall the community to its primary vocation by reminding people why they are here. This is yet another reason why excessive busyness and over-involvement in detail can sometimes be the enemy of wise leadership. If leaders are micromanaging their organizations, not quite doing everyone else's job for them, but always giving the impression that every decision requires their approval or comment, then there is a danger that they will lose sight of the big picture.

In many organizations there is a sense in which the vision is 'given': McDonald's make hamburgers; Ford makes cars; undertakers organize funerals; and schools teach children. As they say, it's not rocket science. It is amazing, however, to see how many organizations lose sight of their reason for being. Only the leader who has a clear sense of the vision, one who is able regularly to step back from the trees in order to see the wood, can lead such an organization.

Do you remember those puzzles that used to be, and still are, very popular in children's comics and puzzle books, where there is a selection of different starting points, a tangled web of interweaving pathways, and a single destination? The idea of the puzzle is to find the correct starting point. You discover this by trial and error, tracing your way along each pathway in turn. But did you ever learn how to cheat at these puzzles? I have to confess to being much too conforming as a child to have ever worked this out for myself. But of course cheating is easy and obvious: you start at the end. By beginning at the finish you can quickly trace your way back to the only correct starting point.

This seems to me to be a perfect image for the sort of leadership that states the obvious and articulates the vision: we start at the end. We do not try to second guess what might happen in the future, but have a clear and defining vision of what the future can be. We then work back from this vision to where we are now in order to discover the right pathway to travel. This won't ever be as easy as some books on management technique and leadership skills like to make out. But unless you have a clear vision of where you want to get to, you will plainly never get there at all.

It is the vision of how things can be at the end that motivates and inspires everything else.

The leader is the guardian and the herald of the vision.

The leader not only articulates the vision but embodies it. Every time the leader speaks it is a recollection of why the organization exists.

Sometimes the vision needs to be discovered or rediscovered. This is why the wise leader is the contemplative person who sets aside time for relaxation and discernment of the big picture. Sometimes, as I have suggested, and as we shall explore in the next chapter, this comes through conversation – the intentional pooling of insights and ideas as we discover together what the vision for the future might be. But in my experience, and in most organizations, there is a vision (even if everyone has forgotten it!). The job of the leader is to remind people.

More problematic is what might be called 'purpose': this is not the vision itself, but the particular pathways that are the right way forwards towards the vision *at this given moment*. In other words, we have the vision, now we have to trace the pathway back to where we are. If we do not, we have little idea of how we might achieve our vision. The leader is the one who works with others to establish what this purpose might be, the one who asks: What route shall we take? What things do we need to do in order to start making this vision real?

If part of our vision as a school is to instil certain values of kindness and selflessness in children, and if at the moment we have particular issues with spitefulness and bullying, then we need to discern a pathway towards that vision that will raise awareness of the issues and cultivate different attitudes in the children. It might be that we will change the way we do assemblies. Or introduce new approaches to daily activities in the classroom. Or monitor behaviour differently at break time. These are purpose questions. If the vision is the mountain top towards which we are travelling, the purpose is the particular pathway we choose to take.

We recognize that there is a choice. There is usually more than one option. But we also recognize our limitations. We have to choose the pathway that we think will be the best. In other words, defining the purpose enables a company or an organization – in this instance a school – to decide what it *isn't going to do* as well as what it is. This is sometimes called pruning – as we observed earlier, sometimes gardening metaphors are the most helpful because of the organic nature of growth and development.

Pruning a plant is not just a matter of cutting back dead wood. This is relatively easy. No, the skilled gardener cuts back living branches in order that the whole plant may be fruitful. If the plant isn't pruned, and if too many fruiting branches are allowed to flourish and compete, then there is a danger that there will be no fruit at all. Judicious discernment and decisive action are needed. The gardener has to be able to say, 'This branch is the one that has the greatest potential for fruitfulness, and therefore this other branch, also healthy and also capable of fruit, must be cut back.'

A great deal of research has demonstrated that healthy organizations tend to do a few things and do them well. They have allowed themselves to be pruned. As well as articulating the vision, the wise and discerning leader will enable the organization to understand its purpose, and then, focusing on this purpose alone, cut back those things in the daily life of the organization that may undermine its fruitfulness.

But it always starts with the vision – how we long for things to be at the end. I am calling this aspect of leadership 'stating the obvious'. It involves the endless recalling of the central vision: something everyone knows about but has so often forgotten. However, as my jumble-sale story illustrates, sometimes this sort of leadership requires the patient development of a process whereby individual stakeholders in the community rediscover the vision for themselves and are therefore better able not only to find the right purpose, but also to commit themselves to taking the steps that reveal themselves to be the right way forward.

And what I have said for the vision of an organization applies equally well to the values. There is no point in being clear about where you want to get to if you have not also considered how you are to travel. These values, which define and shape how we do our business, are principles that the community needs to discern together, so that they are truly a shared manifesto. The job of the leader is to articulate and embody both the vision and the values so that they are transparent in the life that person leads and are also the foundation of everything that happens.

Planning

Vision is the mountain top, the destination we long to reach, and the defining reason that set us out on this journey in the first place. If we are at Ford Motor Cars, then our dream is to make cars; and making the very best cars we can, and enabling the maximum number of people to drive and benefit from our cars, is the mountain top we are travelling towards.

Purpose is the particular pathway up the mountain that we are taking at the moment. Acknowledging our constraints and limitations, we choose which way to go. We recognize that there are other pathways and this one may not be the best. But this is the one we have decided on. We choose to make this car rather than that one. In other words, defining the purpose enables a company or an organization to decide what it isn't going to do as well as what it is. Hence in order to be fruitful we learn how to prune.

Strategy refers to the individual steps that make up the pathway, the actual things we do to achieve the purpose. It is best if the strategy is broken down in such a way that progress can be objectively discerned. It is sometimes said that good strategy has SMART goals. That is, its steps are:

> SPECIFIC
>
> MEASURABLE
>
> AGREED UPON
>
> REALISTIC
>
> TIME BASED.

Alignment is the marshalling of people and resources so that these steps forward are not just identified, but actually taken. Sometimes this means making small, but highly significant, changes to ensure that everything in the organization is working in harmony towards this end and nothing is getting in the way. Billy Connolly has commented that there is no such thing as bad weather, only the wrong clothes. This is a matter of alignment. If it is raining, buy a raincoat!

These four – vision, purpose, strategy and alignment – work together as a model for leadership. It is a model that has been explored and developed in the Oxford Diocese where I now work, and I have found it enormously helpful. The leader is the one who has a special responsibility for articulating the vision and purpose and then ensuring that as many others as possible are exercising their own leadership in renewing the purpose, developing the strategy and aligning the whole organization towards the attainment of the longed-for vision.

Values are the principles that undergird the way you implement your purpose and strategy. Not what you do, but how you do it. They also need to be agreed by everyone and communicated clearly.

chapter 5

SPOILING THE BROTH

> Without counsel, plans go wrong, but with many
> advisers they succeed.
>
> Proverbs 15.22

As every sensible person knows, the broth is spoiled when too many cooks are employed. I want to argue, however, that the Christian vision for leadership is one that is always drawing more people in, helping them discover their gifts, and constantly expanding and sharing leadership.

A first rule of thumb might be this: if you want people to share your vision, get them to help you design it. Your job as the leader is to articulate the vision, but it is not necessarily your job to dream it up. As we noted in the last chapter, often a vision is obvious and given. But sometimes it needs to be worked out. It is always best to involve others in this. When I was stuck in the jumble-sale cycle, getting people to write down why they thought the church existed was a way of helping everyone to reconnect with a vision they knew about, but had forgotten. The leader is the one who dares the whole organization to stop for a minute and take time out to remember why they're here.

Discerning purpose nearly always requires the involvement of everyone. It includes sifting through different options, receiving different insights and ideas, and testing different possibilities. Again, the best leaders are the ones who will be secure enough in themselves to allow this sort of debate to take place. The strategy that emerges is then much more likely to have real ownership and commitment. Not only is this good for the whole organization, it also reduces the likelihood of conflict.

People often feel alienated in their work because they have no stake in the vision and purpose of their company. Valuing the insights and opinions of all may mean that it takes a little longer to agree the purpose and the strategy, but once agreed, there is a much greater likelihood that people will commit themselves to them. And when there is disagreement – as of course there is in every organization – it is less likely to be personality driven. People won't be disagreeing with this or that leader, but with the owned and understood direction and policy of the organization. Disagreement is then less likely to get personal and therefore less likely to get nasty, though of course it still will sometimes. The short cuts of hasty leaders often pave the way for conflict. People feel alienated and left behind and are therefore much more likely to be disruptive if things go wrong.

The best way to handle conflict is to do all that you can to prevent it happening in the first place, but when it does come, to deal with it head on and face to face. And seek to lead in such a way that people are disagreeing with policy, rather than with you personally. This gives you great strength. You do not just have to defend your own hunch, but the agreed strategy of all with whom you live and work. This is transformative for relationships, morale (and output!) within any organization. We are much more likely to work hard and contentedly for something we feel we have a stake in shaping and developing.

But this approach does entail a different attitude to leadership. If you are the sort of person who has hit the ground running, you are much less likely to have consulted and collaborated in the ways that I am suggesting bear much greater fruit. And even if you've started to suspect that you might be moving very rapidly in the wrong direction, you find it almost impossible to change direction for to change would involve admitting you are wrong and that is a vulnerability too far.

We will return to this vital aspect of leadership later on. There are two other things about employing, valuing and trusting too many cooks that we need to look at first: the first is the readiness to take risks (yes, the broth might be spoiled!); and the second is the belief that everyone within the organization or community has gifts to offer and in some sense will exercise leadership.

So let's look at the risky business of taking risks.

If we have already decided that the only worthwhile goal of our enterprise is success, then it follows automatically that the biggest enemy is failure. But if our goal is to enable each member of the organization or community to discover their part within the whole – that is, if we hope to be successful and fruitful, but don't turn that into an idol to which everything else must submit – then it is OK to fail; it is OK to make mistakes; it is OK to take risks.

My favourite story about this goes as follows: a young entre-preneur is employed by a large multinational company. He has an idea that he believes might make some big money. His immediate superior backs him in this venture and he gives it his best shot. But all does not go well. The plan goes belly up and he loses the company several million pounds.

He is called to the office of the Managing Director on the 54th floor. Chastened and dejected, he enters the office, fully expecting to be given the sack. The Managing Director sits him down, talks through the whole sorry business, tries to help him make sense of what has gone wrong and what can be learned from the experience, thanks him for his time and sends him back to his desk.

As he gets up to leave he says to his Managing Director, 'I thought you had brought me up here to give me the sack.'

'The sack!' says the Managing Director incredulously. 'We've just invested several million pounds in your training!'

This is the right attitude to risk and failure – to see it as investment. And part of the investment is time spent learning from what has happened so that lessons can be incorporated into the ever-changing pathways of the future. This Managing Director has not turned success alone into the goal, and is therefore able to respond creatively to failure.

Every organization needs its risk-takers. They are the pioneers who are exercising a form of leadership that is vital for the future health of the organization. If they are abandoned the first time things don't quite go to plan, it is the organization, in the end, that suffers the most. On the assumption that all the gifts of leadership can be carried by one or two people, it has cast aside those who have the pioneering gifts to see what new visions may await us.

Many organizations and communities (not least the Christian Church) lose their way because they have lost their way-finders. These weren't safe company people but pioneers who were often most at home on the edge and on the frontier. Those with ultimate responsibility for leadership, such as the conductor of an orchestra, need to cherish and utilize men and women with these gifts, ensuring that they are protected and valued. This will sometimes mean standing up for those who, by most worldly estimations, have failed for we see that in their failure they have identified paths that should not be taken, thereby getting us one step closer towards discovering the paths that should.

This cherishing of the gifts of others – even if they outshine us in their own areas – is a vital gift of leadership. I have often observed that the most effective leaders are those who don't surround themselves with sycophants and clones, but with challenging, creative people who offer gifts that the leaders themselves don't have.

It is also a matter of humbly acknowledging that everyone has a gift and everyone has a part to play. This is particularly true of leadership in the Church, but has a far wider relevance.

We live in a society that highly prizes some skills but is scornful or ignorant of others. If you have the ability to strike a football with pace and accuracy, you will be richly rewarded. If you have the patience and tenacity to help a small child learn to read or tie up their shoelaces, you won't. That is part of the truly upside-down discrepancies of a society in thrall to market potential.

But what of those who feel they have no talent at all? Some people are far too easily dumped on the scrapheap or left on the shelf. Another role of leadership is to create an environment of encouragement and training rooted in the belief that every person has a vital contribution to make – this not because of some unique talent that just needs to be unearthed, but because each person is precious, regardless of any so-called ability. By valuing someone's contribution, we value them. This enhances all of us and if it means that sometimes the broth is not as tasty as it could be, that won't matter: it will be enjoyed all the more for being the work of every person and not just of a breakaway elite.

I remember some years ago preparing two couples for their wedding. They were similar sorts of people, with similar incomes and working to similar budgets, but they had very different ideas about their wedding receptions. One couple put the *things* of the reception first. They identified what they wanted – in their case, caviar and champagne – and then worked out how many people they could afford to invite, as it turned out, not that many! The other couple put the *people* first. They wrote down who they wanted to come and then worked out what they could afford to offer – in their case, beer and ham sandwiches. But I think I know which reception was the more joyful occasion. I think I know which one valued people the most. I think I know which party was closer to the kingdom of God. I dare to say I think I also know which reception had the tastier food. And it wasn't the one with the champagne and caviar. For these things lose their flavour when they are consumed in isolation, when they become ends in themselves rather than the means whereby we achieve our primary purpose – in this case, a celebration.

Giving leadership away

One of the most remarkable things about Jesus' leadership and ministry was the disproportionate amount of time he gave to a few people. Very early on in his ministry he identifies and calls together a core group through whom his message and his purposes will be known. From then on these are the people he spends the most time with. He is leading leaders.

In the Church of England many clergy feel that they must strive to be equally available to all people all of the time. This of course is impossible. Once you are with one person you are by definition unavailable to everyone else. Out of a desire to be fair and impartial, many Anglican clergy spread themselves extremely thinly.

All we can say is that this is not what Jesus did. In fact it is amazing, once we have cottoned on to this, to see how unavailable Jesus is a lot of the time – disappearing off on his own, even hiding from the disciples, but always willing to give them additional time as they need it.

I'm sure other Churches suffer from the same well-intentioned and equitable distribution of time. I reckon a good many other organizations do too. But the secret of effective leadership here seems to involve having an eye on a larger goal: the affirmation, training and mobilization of others. In which case, one of the main tasks of leadership is to identify and nurture those who will not only take the organization forward but in due course take it over.

If you have implanted in the DNA of the organization this constant recruitment and affirmation of others, then it will indeed cascade out into every department, creating an environment of trust, care and facilitation. Everyone will be cared for. And everyone will be entrusted with the exercise of their own gifts and leadership. But it will have come from the nature of the organization rather than just from the ever-diminishing and constantly overworked resources of one person. In fact there is no other way of doing it effectively. The leader has to model what the organization must become.

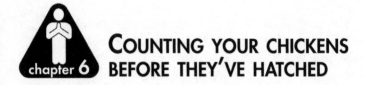

COUNTING YOUR CHICKENS
chapter 6 **BEFORE THEY'VE HATCHED**

> By wisdom a house is built, and by understanding it is established; by knowledge the rooms are filled with all precious and pleasant riches.
>
> Proverbs 24.3-4

Sometimes the vision is too small. I remember talking to a youth worker some years ago. He was just starting out, and was fired up with great aspirations for helping young people. Working in a deprived and challenging context, he wanted to help young people regain self-esteem, discover dignity, and get on in life. When I met him again, five years into the job, he seemed to have settled for something else. The big vision of changed lives had been replaced with a child-minding service for bored teenagers.

But this doesn't just happen to youth workers. It is a danger in every occupation. The vision shrinks to fit the reality. We fail to trace a pathway from where we are to where we want to be.

So keep your vision big.

The chickens may not have hatched yet.

Perhaps the eggs have not even been laid.

Spur yourself on with a ridiculously large vision of how things could be: one that is beyond human imagining; one that seems inconceivably huge but gloriously attractive; one that is for ever drawing on the talents and abilities of those involved; and, crucially, one that is able to manage change and make changes in order to get to where you want to be. As the Bible rightly warns us: Where there is no vision, the people perish.

When I first became a bishop people would often ask me: 'What is your vision?' I always replied, 'I don't have one!' This was not what they were expecting, but it was another way of shaking people out of the attitude that thinks vision belongs to one person – the mighty leader – rather than being both a gift from beyond us and a creation from within us. This is why I am drawn to the upside-down logic that counts chickens before they hatch and dreams the kind of absurd abundance that was so irritatingly powerful in some of the parables of Jesus.

Famously, Jesus speaks about a sower going out to sow. The sower is clearly incompetent, and any of Jesus' first listeners, all of them peasant farmers who knew all there was to know about the careful and diligent sowing of seed, especially in such a difficult and unforgiving climate, would have been incensed that this idle and irresponsible fellow should have had such a copious crop. Some fell on the path! What rubbish – any decent sower would not have been be so wasteful with the seed! Some fell among thorns! How ridiculous – any sensible sower would have carefully prepared the ground! Some were snaffled up by birds! Inconceivable! Where was the scarecrow? Jesus' listeners would have snorted with laughter when he suggested that this bungling sower should be rewarded with such a mighty yield.

But Jesus is deliberately speaking of an abundance that is beyond our deserving. Something that is not dependent on our wisdom or effort. Something that is beyond our imagining. We are not supposed to draw the lesson that we do not need to work. Sensible farmers still have to dig the earth, remove the weeds and water the soil. But beyond this, on the other side of our sensible and cautious expectations, lies a bigger vision. Something that confounds logic. Something that is much more than the sum of its parts. Something that transcends the usual predictions.

Those of us working in the Church always need to be motivated and inspired by this vision, which is both beyond us and yet, at the same time, conceived in our midst. But I also think that this same profligate hugeness can benefit any organization. Let us dream a vision that stretches beyond our usual horizons. Of course, we will not get there all at once. Of course, there will be a sense in which such a vision always remains beyond us. But let us not settle for a small vision, one that fails to inspire or terrify.

We are at our best when we are amazed by what is set beyond us and before us. It makes us more likely to get down to the painstaking business of working out the particular pathways we need to follow to get towards this vision – our purpose, and the individual steps we need to take, all those little decisions that make up the everyday leading and management of the organization or community we lead.

Leaders are the guardians of this vision. They may not be the authors – though this will often be the case – but they are the ones who are continually raising people's sights and stretching their expectations. At the same time, the leaders need to be the people who are developing the strategy to make it happen and rolling up their sleeves to make specific and strategic contributions on the front line. Healthy organizations today will not necessarily have neat chains of command where the leader simply delegates lesser tasks down the line. The best leaders will make their contribution in a number of different ways: first of all ensuring that the vision and purpose are there, but then also being the people who are prepared to get stuck into some of the most menial tasks if that is where the effort is required and especially if that is a way of encouraging and motivating others.

Incidentally, getting stuck in is often the way the vision is renewed and expanded. In any organization, some of the most important insights are gained from those doing the most menial tasks or those who are newest to the job. They see things differently. They see things that the leader sometimes misses. The newest person will often have the freshest perspective. Hence leaders in today's fast-moving and rapidly changing context cannot lose touch with those in the front line. They need to be free of too much day-to-day stuff so that they are able to rove freely through the organization and make their contribution in a number of different ways. Thus they guard and develop the vision; ensure that the purpose – the direction of the organization – is being maintained; and actually contribute their energy and expertise to some of the particular steps being taken.

Leading an organization or community today is therefore much more like steering a ship in choppy waters than like driving a car down a motorway. On the motorway things are fairly straightforward. The road is mapped out before you. The traffic may be fast or slow but steering is not really a problem. At sea it is very different. As any sailor will tell you, the irony of navigating a course at sea is that although you can draw a line on a map connecting A to B, in order to get there you will have to make many different changes of direction as wind and current shift around you.

The German theologian Hans Küng has said that to do the same thing while everything else around you changes is not to do the same thing. In other words, if the wind has changed, it is no use trying to steer the same course and expect to reach the same destination. A leader who is too far removed from the deck, unable to feel the change of wind, let alone hear the cries of the sailors in the rigging, will soon end up leading in the wrong direction. The tragedy will be that the course has stayed the same. It will be everything else – all those uncontrollable things around you – that will have shifted you.

This has always been true, but it becomes more and more of an issue in the type of world we now inhabit. For the Church this has meant uncomfortable changes in recent years, and it requires a deftness of touch, a largeness of vision, a cool head and a good team around you, if you are to navigate well.

Let me offer an illustration of this type of leadership.

A couple of years ago Jamie Oliver, the TV celebrity chef, had the ridiculous vision of transforming the way schoolchildren ate. He wanted to radically change school dinners. The story of this unfolding vision – the pathways he chose and the steps he took – was told in a fascinating TV series: *Jamie's School Dinners.*

As Jamie Oliver worked out how to reach this goal, his very big vision found a very tight focus. He began in one school, training one school dinner lady to cook differently. It was a struggle. This was not what she was used to. Initially, many of the children rejected the new food, pining for the 'chips with everything' that had been taken from them. But they persevered. Jamie was sustained by the vision. After a while the dinner lady caught the vision too. The food improved. The children's expectations changed. Progress was made. And from this first small step enormous other strides were taken. Presently a whole London borough was feeding its children differently.

Along the way Jamie had to reinvent some wheels (more of this later). He discovered that his preconceived ideas had to be set aside as he worked out, on the ground, what a new, healthier, but still affordable, school dinner might look like. He had to learn how to teach others to produce it. And how to produce it on a massive scale and within budget.

There were also times when the personal cost of the whole venture became painfully clear. This is also something we will look at later on.

For me, the highlight of the series was several episodes in, when Jamie took a whole army of dinner ladies to an army boot camp and trained them himself in the fine art of the new healthy option. This really was too many cooks counting too many chickens!

I know some people think that celebrity chefs are impossibly irritating, but I found *Jamie's School Dinners* wonderfully inspiring. Jamie Oliver embodied an engaging style of leadership. He was articulating an astonishing vision. But he had also worked out, and was working out – to the last detail – the different steps that were needed to get towards it. At one and the same time he was the visionary idealist and the very hands-on practitioner. He was leading from the front and the back at the same time. He had one eye on the horizon and another on the tiniest detail that he alone might have the capacity to change. He had one hand on the tiller and another in the hands of those who would go on to lead others. It is a way of leading that is worth following!

And all the time he was being inspired and motivated by the crazy profligacy of a huge vision. This was what led him. He was not leading out of a desire to lead, but out of a desire to see the vision accomplished, something that was good in itself and that on the way would transform the lives of many others. Henri Nouwen has observed that the Church – and the world – need leaders who know how to be led.

How does change happen?

Whole books have been written on this subject; here is a very modest contribution. It seems to me that the following things need to be in place for change to be managed creatively:

A clearly owned and articulated vision and purpose
All that we have said about designing and articulating vision and being clear about purpose is absolutely vital for managing change. If the vision is just one person's idea, it will either fail or be pushed through so reluctantly that it will never bear fruit.

Checking people's commitment When making decisions about change, it is just as important to find out who has the energy to implement something as to know whether or not people agree with it. There are plenty of proposals I agree with, but that does not necessarily mean I will have the energy or time to make them happen. As my former colleague James Lawrence used to say, when someone says they agree to something it could mean, 'Yes, I agree, and I will give my life to making this happen.' Alternatively, it could mean: 'How much longer is this meeting going on? We've already discussed this for over an hour. For goodness sake, let's just make a decision. I agree.' If too many people's agreement is in the latter category, nothing much will ever happen.

An agreed strategy It is no good having the bright idea, or even agreeing to act upon it, if time has not also been given to deciding how it will be implemented. Those with responsibility for leadership must ensure that the actual steps are in place not just for the decision to be made, but for the decision to be implemented.

Setting real priorities What are you going to stop doing in order to implement this new suggestion? So many organizations just add to an already overcrowded agenda without ever daring to consider what could be stopped: not because it is bad, but because time, money and energy are limited.

Timing The scriptures speak about seasons of fruitfulness.

Sometimes the idea is right, but the time isn't. Sometimes this is to do with critical mass. If enough people care enough about the same thing at the same time, then it will probably get done. Sometimes the job of the leader is to discern the right time. But of course sometimes it is also the leader's job to be prophetic and to stand outside the mass of popular opinion and do everything possible to direct people's energies towards a goal that is presently out of sight to most of them.

Caring for those who have most to lose With any real change in an organization there will be some who are left behind and some who feel they have lost out. Anticipating who these people will be and offering them care *before the change takes place* is not only the best way of honouring their disagreement, but also of preventing them from derailing the change. In many organizations, and especially the Church, change is held back because a few people hold the leadership to ransom. Or else real change is never even considered out of fear of this backlash. Being clear that some people will not like it; ensuring that the vision and strategy are owned by the leadership; offering genuine care for those who may feel left behind: this is the only real approach to managing change in a way that is not only true to the purpose – that is, ensuring that the change actually takes place – but also true to the values – taking seriously the well-being and contribution of every member.

REINVENTING THE WHEEL

chapter 7

> Iron sharpens iron, and one person sharpens the wits of another. Anyone who tends a fig tree will eat its fruit . . .
>
> Proverbs 27.17-18a

In the past 20 years a great number of courses have been produced to help adults become Christians (I am the author of one of them, so I'm not knocking them) and a few years ago a survey was conducted to find out which course was the most effective.

Surely the all-conquering *Alpha* course with its glossy publicity, smooth presentation and national advertising would come out on top? Or perhaps the more inclusive educational methodology of its rival, *Emmaus*, would triumph? What about one of the others with their snazzy DVDs or interactive web sites? No, the winner was a surprise to most people.

The survey found that all the published courses were pretty much on a par. You pays your money and you makes your choice. They all did a good and fairly similar job, you just needed to find the one that suited you best (and then adapt it like mad – though it rarely says this on the tin). But one course did seem to be significantly more effective. One did stand out against the others. When asked how many people who had attended the course went on to become members of the Church, this course had a higher rate of hits. Its name? Well, there wasn't one: not that anyone would recognize. The reason? It was the home-made course from a single parish that was included in the survey as an afterthought. And where can you buy it? Well, you can't. The whole point of the home-made course is that it is home-made. Bucking the trend, confounding the expectations of all those who think that bigger is better and that answers can be found on the shelf, this course was written and produced by those who were going to run it. They owned it. And although its content was probably very similar to that of the published courses, people's commitment to it was greater. This was what made the difference. People had put themselves into it. And you are much more likely to invite others to a course that you have had a hand in producing than to one you have bought from a catalogue. You are going to have much more confidence in it. You are going to stick with it and stick at it when the going gets tough. It is what I am calling a reinvented wheel.

In the life of most organizations, there are many situations when, as resources are being looked for and plans are being considered, and an idea begins to emerge, someone will interrupt saying, 'We don't need to reinvent the wheel.' And usually such an interruption is greeted with nodding heads and general agreement. So much so that the person whose idea has been so effectively squashed rather wishes they had never suggested anything in the first place, especially something so apparently obvious that someone else has already produced it and they were clearly too dim to have noticed.

Well, let me disagree. When someone says we shouldn't reinvent the wheel, I think that nine times out of ten the appropriate answer is, 'Yes, we should!' Because then it will be your wheel. You will have designed it. You will have thought it through. You will have grappled with the issues and the problems. You will have worked out how to use it. You will have committed to it at a much deeper level. You will have owned it.

It may take longer. And the finished product may not be as sleek and shiny as other wheels. It may not even be as good. But reinventing the wheel doesn't mean you cannot look at other people's designs or learn from their wisdom and experience. To insist that you can reinvent the wheel is a way of issuing a warning against a knee-jerk reaction that says it is a sin to reinvent wheels and that results in our going for someone else's wheel, which may not actually fit.

You wouldn't say to a child writing their first poem, 'Oh, don't bother yourself with that, Shakespeare already had the last word on poems centuries ago.' Nor would you say to an adult taking up a new pursuit, be it water-colour painting, car mechanics or conversational French: 'Someone else has already done it better than you, therefore there's no point in continuing, just buy their product and move on.' No, the process of discovery, creativity, trial and error is good in itself and is part of a larger process whereby we not only learn to make the wheel, but in due course learn to make better wheels, that fit a given situation more precisely.

The wheel that you need may be only very subtly different from someone else's, but you will never find this out until you have gone through the painstaking process of working out your own solutions to your own problems. It is because so many organizations don't reinvent the wheel that they look so decidedly wonky. It is a lovely wheel. But it doesn't quite fit.

But this way of leading and planning requires another mind shift and another great dollop of forgotten wisdom. First, we need to recognize and honour the capacity we have to invent and reinvent. Solutions are not commodities that we can buy off the shelf. The fancy packaging of shop-bought products may be alluring, but they rarely deliver what they promise. In fact they tie us into a cycle of consuming where we are endlessly on the lookout for the next big thing, which is actually a quick fix that doesn't quite work. We human beings are wonderfully creative. The plea to avoid reinventing the wheel can sometimes smother creativity – just as someone has an idea, the idea is rejected. We are far too quickly shifted into unreflective, frantic, 'go out and buy it' mode. In my experience, it is usually much better to jump in quick and suggest that reinventing wheels is precisely what we are in business for!

Secondly, you will therefore need a commitment to the long term. This way of working rarely yields instant results. But in breaking out of the addiction to endless short-term, so-called solutions we will leave the bandwagon behind for good; and with a greater commitment to the wheel we have reinvented we are more likely to find the right solutions (and therefore the fruitful ones).

On the way we will have honoured and encouraged the creative ingenuity of those with whom we are working: especially those precious people who have ideas and want to try new things. Rather than being stifled, they will be set free. They will have space in which their gifts and their leadership can be utilized. Reinventing wheels is therefore good for morale as well as productivity. But it takes longer. You will have to kneel down for a bit as you puzzle out how to make something that hitherto you have always bought off a shelf.

The consumer society with its competing brands vying for attention is not only idolatrous, it is demeaning. A more reflective and contemplative approach to leadership breaks out of this malaise. We trust our ability to find solutions by trusting the people we have been given. Ideas are allowed to germinate and, if appropriate, bear fruit. We stop looking over our shoulders all the time at what other people are doing, fantasizing that there is a 'solution' out there that someone else has discovered and that we just need to find and buy, no matter how many changes of direction it requires, how much money is wasted and how much creativity is squandered or neglected.

Try it! Next time someone says we shouldn't reinvent the wheel, disagree. Give it a go. Reinvent that wheel and see where it takes you.

This attitude to invention, reinvention and trusting the creativity of those around you also re-enforces the point about change that I was making in the last chapter. Very often the changes we need to make are forced upon us because of other changes happening around us. Hence we face the paradox that to stay the same we have to change; to continue in the same direction we have to change course. If we are always reliant on the solutions of others and if we fail to trust our own creativity and the creativity of those around us, then we are less likely to be able to make that difficult decision to tack against the wind in order to stay on course. This is where leaders really are paid to lead. The courage we need to stand still and test the wind, and to seek out the horizon through the mist and fog of competing agendas and demands, is the same courage that trusts others, shares leadership and only does those things that only we can do.

Part of the process of reinvention is therefore the reinvention of yourself. No one else can tell you how to be a leader. Of course, you must seek advice and must constantly allow yourself to be appraised, but leadership is not one of those things you can learn from a book. Hence in writing this one I'm trying not to sound too prescriptive, but to point you in some right directions where you can discover for yourself and reinvent the wheel of your leadership. In the next chapter we will deal with some of these very personal, and costly, aspects of leading.

Making difficult decisions

Perhaps the hardest thing about being a leader is finding that the buck stops on your desk. There is no way of avoiding this. It is part of the reason why leaders can sometimes feel lonely. But many leaders deal with these situations in one of two equally unhelpful ways. They either become more and more dictatorial, making lots of decisions, enjoying the illusion of power and the status their position brings, but not necessarily achieving anything. Or else they abdicate responsibility, fail to make decisions, talk of consensus, while creating a vacuum where nothing much takes place, or where lots of competing and conflicting things are allowed to happen. Either way, the organization flounders and everyone just waits for you to fall so that they can replace you with a different leader (though, sadly, in some organizations the pendulum just swings from one dysfunctional mode of leadership to another). The middle way – the sort of upside-down way that I am extolling – involves two clear principles:

Only do what only you can do Be clear about your own priorities and responsibilities. Trust and delegate everything else. This ability to trust and this confidence in one's own role as leader are nurtured by the sort of contemplation this book encourages.

And when you do make the decisions that only you can make, *ensure that they arise from and are consistent with the agreed vision and values of the organization.* In other words, although it is you who must make the decision, the decision must clearly reflect the organization you lead.

chapter 8

SHEDDING THE THICK SKIN

Happy is the one who is never without fear, but one who is hard-hearted will fall into calamity.

Proverbs 28.14

Of all the upside-down wisdom that the Christian Church offers to the world (and has so often forgotten itself), perhaps the greatest is that the leader should so embody the purposes and values of the organization that he feels the pain more keenly than anyone else.

When I was younger and much less experienced I kept on hoping (expecting?) that one day I would miraculously grow the thick skin that other people spoke of as being so necessary. I would often find myself getting hurt. Sometimes it was because I was over-involved. But often it just seemed that being involved had to mean sharing the feelings that were around: therefore there was no alternative to getting hurt, except quitting. People told me that I ought to learn detachment and a proper professional disengagement – and there is wisdom here that I want to explore – but often they just said I ought to grow the skin of a rhinoceros. But this never happened, and even as I did learn detachment, it could never be to the extent that I was not in tune with the feelings and concerns around me. I was investing myself in this enterprise of leading a church. If I was entitled to feel the joy of its delights, then I couldn't avoid the pain of its discomforts. I thought time might change things. But it hasn't. My skin has remained stubbornly thin.

Well, here we are tiptoeing into a minefield and I fear that of all the crazy things I've shared with you in this book this is where I am most likely to be misunderstood. Yes, it is important to be detached. Just as you can't and shouldn't try to micromanage any organization you are leading, so you can't and shouldn't get involved with every person's life or in trying to sort out every conflict or problem. As the organization or community develops, so there should be proper areas of responsibility with boundaries around them, and part of the job of creating a happy, functioning team is to draw those boundaries carefully, communicate them clearly and observe them diligently.

By 'feeling the pain' I do not mean getting over-involved and overextended in every aspect of the community's life. Nor do I mean becoming some sort of doormat where everyone else wipes off their problems. Detachment is important. However committed we are to an enterprise – even the Church – we need to distinguish between our role in the organization and our own sense of ourselves, independent from it.

I am not my job. Even those of us with so-called vocations, need to make a distinction between our personal and professional personas. Hence there have been numerous occasions in recent years when, facing a difficult situation, I have found myself saying, 'Stephen, you need to remember this is a job for the Bishop for Reading.' In other words, there is, and needs to be, a separation of who I am in myself and with my family and in my leisure, from who I am in the work that I do, however committed I am to it. This is not to say I am two people. I am one person who has responsibilities and vocations in different areas. Some overlap is inevitable. Some is desirable. But if all the roles conflate into one, then I am actually more likely to lose who I am. It is rarely a sign of integration. Usually it is a sign of one part of a life so dominating everything else that the proper concerns of rest and leisure are squeezed out. As I have been at pains to emphasize, wise leaders need time out. A balanced life of leisure, rest, reflection and work is most likely to be the most fruitful life.

No, what I am speaking about here is the nature of commitment. The Church has been dogged by a certain sort of professional-ization, which it has sometimes adopted rather uncritically from the world, and which is almost scornful of anyone who so cares about their work that they feel the pain of its concerns. In this approach to leadership, balance and detachment become blinkered tunnel vision and remote isolation. 'What can I get out?' replaces 'What can I put in?'

Because the leader is called to embody the values and purposes of the organization, the leader must be the one who knows when the organization is hurting. As I said above, you cannot expect to share the delights if you are not prepared to feel the pain. The desirability of thick skin therefore becomes very dubious indeed. Rather, I need to hope for a way of working where I can at the same time be properly detached, so that I preserve my sense of self and remain fresh and focused in my responsibilities, and be so committed that I am able constantly to check the pulse of what is going on. In other words, I need to listen to the heartbeat of the community I am leading. I also need to be leading in a way that ensures that the goal of the organization is not conflicting with the values. Such conflicts inevitably come along from time to time and are sometimes the cause of the biggest hurt. The leader has to manage them.

Let me give you one very small example. One of the values of the football team my youngest son plays for is that everybody who wants to be part of the team gets to play, and although the manager wants the team to win, giving everyone a chance to participate is just as important. Consequently, from my position on the sidelines I have on numerous occasions watched matches in which, with perhaps fifteen minutes to go, and the team maybe a goal ahead and the players on the pitch gelled well together and looking as if they can maintain their lead, the manager has nevertheless rotated the squad, deliberately bringing on players who he knows are not as good as those they are replacing. In this way he is demonstrating by his actions the values that the team espouses and in so doing is articulating the vision. The players want to win, but not at all costs and certainly not at the cost of the values that make the team such a joy to be part of.

It is not easy to lead this sort of team. It requires a different sort of leadership. The boys want to win the match. They know that some players are better than others. They are sometimes angry at the manager's decisions (as, indeed, are some of the parents on the touchline!). But this is a leadership with integrity that is guarding the values of the community and balancing this goal with all the others.

I am also moved that this manager is not ashamed of showing his feelings from time to time. I have seen him shed a tear in front of the boys when a much loved member of the team moves on.

The same sort of leadership is seen in a family where the parents don't just tell the children what it is that is expected of them, but try to live it out themselves.

What I am saying is that this sort of leadership is required in all organizations. By embodying the vision, and being vulnerable to the pain that inevitably comes with any leadership of anything that matters, we acquire those vital ingredients that cannot be obtained in any other way: integrity and authenticity. We have what people sometimes call a good heart.

It is this sort of heart that needs guarding and nourishing if we are to lead well.

In the Old Testament there is a beautiful passage in which the prophet Ezekiel speaks of God giving a new heart to his people. Their old heart of stone will be removed. Their lives will be changed. I am interpreting 'heart of stone' to mean what we might call a thick skin: a way of living that is impervious to the influence of others. We cannot feel people's pain because we never listen to what they have to say. We have become entirely self-absorbed and self-referential. The only ideas that matter are our own. We can no longer be taught.

Ezekiel obviously expects us to understand his words in terms of our relationship with God, but our relationship with others and, indeed, our relationship with the vision that originally inspired us can equally become characterized by such fossilization. Our attitudes harden. Perhaps we have been hurt once too often. We stop listening and we stop learning. We stop moving. We stop changing. All of a sudden we have atrophied.

What we need in these situations is a change of heart, but what the Bible promises is not what we might necessarily expect: 'I will remove from your body the heart of stone', says the prophet, 'and give you . . .', well, what would you like instead? Most of us would probably plump for a 'super bionic, never-to-be-broken-again' heart. That would seem a most desirable thing to have. But no, the promise is this: 'and give you a heart of flesh' (Ezekiel 36.26). I will give you a heart that is better able to feel the pain of others because it is better able to enter into relationship with them. As Rowan Williams has observed: 'If we refuse to be flesh, we become less than human.'[1]

The greatest leaders have this sort of heart. They feel the anguish of others; they empathize with their pain; they strive towards the mountain top of a vision that continually inspires and provokes them. And they maintain this heart of flesh by ensuring that they are properly detached from the intricacies of their organization so that they neither overwhelm others nor are overwhelmed themselves; and also by trusting others, knowing that what matters is the vision they pursue not their own status or position; and by regularly and intentionally allowing themselves to be evangelized by that vision. They make themselves vulnerable to it. They let it cheer them and chide them.

Think of Nelson Mandela or Václav Havel or Martin Luther King or any truly great leader: they touched the hearts of others and led the whole world towards astonishing changes of heart because

---

[1] Rowan Williams, *Open to Judgement: Sermons and Addresses,* Darton, Longman & Todd, 1994, p. 42.

they empathized and embodied the heart of the concern that aroused them, rebuked them and led them on. They had a restlessness that would not let them put the vision down. But they also had a selflessness that was continually being nourished by their vulnerability to other people's hearts. They had what is sometimes called emotional intelligence. This is hard to define but describes the capacity not only to handle your own emotions well, but also to recognize and understand and help manage the emotions of others around you. It is about self-awareness and self-motivation, but it is also about taking into account the moods and feelings of others. Managing these relationships is just as vital for the success of an enterprise as all the other component parts that usually receive much greater attention.

To extol the virtues of thick skin is often just an excuse to disregard feelings. It is a recipe for disaster. Not only will the enterprise itself be far more likely to succeed if people's feelings are properly considered and managed, but you, the leader, are far less likely to be stressed or strained.

The conscious and intentional preservation of thin skin is not a sign of weakness or naivety but a sign of emotional intelligence, the acceptance of the offer of a new heart – a heart of flesh – one that is in tune with the vision and in touch with those the vision serves.

It is obviously vital that Christian leaders should have this sort of servant heart. But it seems to me that this is an area where almost every leader has much to learn. At the very basic level of competence and output, your organization is more likely to flourish if you are in touch with people's feelings and take them into account in all your decision-making. On the blue-sky, big-picture level of vision-building and scenario-planning, leaders who are in touch with their own feelings, in tune with others, and are constantly allowing themselves to be led, are more likely to come up with the most creative ways forward or at least be most open to the person who has glimpsed the way.

This is how people lead when they hit the ground kneeling.

They are not ashamed or diminished by their vulnerability.

They are not in thrall to the agendas and emotional deceptions of others.

They are neither swayed by people's moods nor ignorant of the importance of taking them into account.

They are not self-seeking or unduly self-reliant. They have a proper sense of their own responsibility to lead, but they never imagine it is not a responsibility to be shared, indeed, to be given away.

They know their own mind, but part of this is knowing when to change it.

They know their gifts, and use them wisely, sparingly and strategically, always wanting to build up the gifts of others. They nurture new possibilities and they cross new frontiers. They employ people around them who have gifts they could never dream of possessing themselves. They are succoured by the creativity of others. They long to kindle creativity in everyone.

For them, the values of the organization are as important as the vision. The two are tied together. The way they travel is as important as the destination they seek. They are the real thing. They have that rare but instantly recognizable quality that we call authenticity. It is this that gives them authority. Not the medals on the chest, not the sign above the door, not the salary in the bank, not an abstract appeal to something beyond themselves, but something that pulses within them and is visible in all they say and do, something that is written in their heart.

Leaders who hit the ground kneeling are kneeling before a vision that they long to make a reality. It is this that nourishes and guides them. It is this they return to, and it is because of this that they can let go of themselves in order to serve a higher agenda. They don't need to take themselves too seriously – it is the mountain top of the vision that matters. But they take others seriously, never separating them and their needs from the causes they follow.

They can laugh at themselves and be relaxed and fresh in the midst of the stickiest situations. They know where their affirmation is coming from. They embody the values they espouse. And they are not so stupid as to imagine they will never get it wrong, or too stubborn to admit it. A thin skin has given them a good heart, one that is constantly being refreshed and reaffirmed.

In the choppiest water theirs are the steadiest hands on the tiller.

Their eyes are fixed on the horizon and they are determined and reliable enough to carry on taking one toilsome tack at a time.

They are focused, but rarely frantic.

They are industrious, but not busy.

They get things done, but not only do they always exalt the efforts of the team, they lead in such a way that the team themselves genuinely feel that the work was theirs.

And of course it was. The team were well led. They were led by a leader whose concern was the destination not the plaque on the door.

Leadership like this is not really learned in a book. Not even this one! This just gives you a few hints and, hopefully, a desire to lead well.

This sort of leadership is learned by reflecting deeply on your own motivations, on your own passions, on the examples of others who have led you and on a steady and regular resetting of the compass of your vision through contemplation and reflection.

It is the sort of leadership that is best modelled by Jesus himself. On the one hand, he seems an impossible role model. On the other, Christians have always believed that Jesus shows us what being human is supposed to be like; and they believe that with God's help this is a way of living – and a way of leading – that we should all aspire to. Whether or not you are a Christian, I hope that this little book may have helped you rethink what the Church has to offer the world of leadership and of how you yourself go about leading.

The servant leader

What was the greatest example of leadership that Jesus offered? Well, it was probably on the night before he died. In St John's Gospel we are told that Jesus knows that God has placed all things into his hands and that he has come from God and is returning to God. In other words, Jesus is conscious of the divine commission that is his and his alone. He has a job to do, a lonely, painful and difficult job, and he now needs to communicate this to his followers, that little band of miscreants and misfits through whom his purpose and values will be known. How does he do this? How does he let them know who he is and how his leadership will be expressed?

He rises from the table. He lays aside his outer garments. He takes a towel and a basin of water. He washes his disciples' feet. The final example of his leadership is one of service. He is secure in himself and in the affirmation and service he has received. And so he gives service to others. He shows them that true leadership means to serve. He hits the ground kneeling.

chapter 9

A FINAL THOUGHT

Keep your heart with all vigilance, for from it flow
the springs of life.

Proverbs 4.23

It was G. K. Chesterton who said that if a job's worth doing it's
worth doing badly. And I think it was Quentin Crisp who said that
if at first you don't succeed, perhaps failure is your thing.

In a book of upside-down wisdom I want to give these two great
wits the last word.

G. K. Chesterton is right: if something is worth doing it's worth
doing. Of course, you do it to the very best of your ability, but it is
not your excellence that decides the value of the enterprise. It is
worth doing whether or not you do it well. It is worth persevering
even if there are others who can do it better than you. It is your
attitude that matters not your excellence. Hit the ground kneeling
and your attitude is more likely to be right: and at the very least
you will not have taken yourself too seriously, nor imagined that
you are the saviour of the world. You will have carried on being
able to laugh at yourself and the woeful inadequacy of your
efforts. All this is vital for healthy leadership. It will save you from
at best becoming a colossal bore, at worst a tyrant.

And Quentin Crisp is right. If what you are doing is worth while, if you
are persevering to the best of your ability, if the vision that inspires

you is worth the investment of your work, your gifts, your energy, your soul, then don't make success into a god. Keep on keeping on. Do not be deterred by failure. Do not stop at the first hurdle. Be prepared to fall off many times. What we are seeking is worth seeking. The vision is worth pursuing whether or not we get there.

The things that are really worth while in life are rarely easy. And travelling well is just as important as arriving, shrewdly discerning the right destination as important as moving. More so: it is easy to go the wrong way.

So check your bearings. Feel the direction of the wind: not necessarily to follow it, but to tack against it if you have to. Decide how you must travel and set your compass afresh. Hit the ground kneeling and you will have *time* to do this. Hit the ground kneeling and you will have the *ability* to do this. Hit the ground kneeling and you will have the *capacity* to do this. Hit the ground kneeling and your heart will be refreshed. And whether or not you achieve excellence, whether or not you are successful, it will have been worth it.

The parable of the trees revisited

Each chapter of this book has opened with a short quotation from the book of Proverbs. This book is part of the wisdom tradition of the Old Testament, a body of writings that encourages us to live with complexity and to ponder on the experience of others without pretending that there are simple customized answers to intricate and multifaceted questions. In this way we grow in wisdom; not by pulling answers off the shelf but by inhabiting a tradition of which we can become a part.

This is a different way of going about things for many people today. We like quick answers and we prize instant solutions. But they don't work. A quick fix here creates a slow-burning bungle somewhere else.

We have much to learn from the past. We do this by opening up a dialogue between the experience of the past – in this case, the accumulated wisdom of the Christian tradition, its stories and its conclusions – and the questions and experiences we face today. The answer that we then find for ourselves – a reinvented wheel if you like – is much better than the answer we are given by others. Even if it ends up looking very similar, it will actually be much more effective.

Right at the beginning of the book – though you may have passed over it quickly – is a passage from the book of Judges entitled 'The parable of the trees'. Before you put this book away, have another look at it. What does it mean? What does it tell you about the vocation to lead and the inter-relatedness of different gifts and callings? What upside-down wisdom does it point to? How does it help shape your vocation to lead? Dwell in the story for a little while. Do with it what this book says all leaders must do with life. Contemplate it. Reflect upon it. See where it leads.

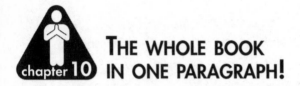

THE WHOLE BOOK
chapter 10 **IN ONE PARAGRAPH!**

> The faithful will abound with blessings, but one who
> is in a hurry to be rich will not go unpunished.
>
> Proverbs 28.20

Wise leadership flows from contemplation. The best leaders are not busy but focused. They are not in a hurry. Getting it right is better than getting it quick. They only do what only they can do. They articulate and guard the vision and values of the organization. They are faithful to it. They involve others. They trust them. They delegate and share leadership. They are prepared to be followers themselves. Their goal is the well-being of those whom they serve and achieving the goals of the organization. Because rest, reflection and recreation are priorities, they see the big picture and they model for others a balanced and healthy lifestyle. This makes for good team-building and this enables creative change to take place. They reinvent wheels so that they have ones that fit precisely. They foster crazy visions, counting their chickens before they hatch. And because they value the contribution of everyone, they don't mind risking the possible spoiling of the broth. They take what they are doing seriously, but they don't take themselves too seriously. They are able to laugh and they are able to cry. They care for those who are left behind. They feel the pain when things go wrong. They are good listeners. They have thin skins and abundant hearts. They build consensus but are not afraid of making decisions when they have to – decisions, though, that always reflect the agreed vision and values of their community. Because of this, people's gifts are valued and developed and the scope of the organization extended. Creative people work around them and for them. Things get done. Everyone says they have done it themselves. They are right. Good leaders build effective teams. The best leaders make themselves redundant.

A bigger yes

And if after all this you still have trouble saying no (like many of us), and if you still feel that your life is run by other people's agendas, enjoy this final thought: What is your big yes? In that area of life where you exercise leadership, what is the one thing, more than any other, that you feel called to? Sit still and contemplate this, the biggest stone of all: and then when you know your big yes, all those other little nos might fall into place.

And if even this fails, remember the story of the bishop who went to see his spiritual director and told him all his troubles. The wise spiritual guide sat back in his chair and advised the bishop to sleep more.

'Why?' asked the bishop.

'It will limit your opportunity to do further damage,' came the reply.